The
CAT
PUZZLER

PATRICIA KING

summersdale

THE CAT PUZZLER

Summersdale Publishers Ltd

Copyright © Fine Folio Publishing Ltd, 2012

Text copyright © Patricia King, 2012

Summersdale Publishers Ltd
46 West Street
Chichester
West Sussex
PO19 1RP
UK

www.summersdale.com

Printed and bound in China

ISBN: 978-1-84953-287-7

PRODUCED BY
Fine Folio Publishing Limited
6 Bourne Terrace, Bourne Hill, Wherstead,
Ipswich, Suffolk, IP2 8NG, UK

FOREWORD

My involvement with cats goes back to my early family life in South America, England and Europe, when my father named our family cats after Royal Navy ships.

Every year thousands of people open their homes to a new cat, and these graceful and beautiful animals give endless hours of pleasure and delight, but never surrender their independence. They are steeped in history, from being worshipped as deities and protectors of temples to being regarded as witches' familiars. They are featured in nursery rhymes, proverbs and folklore, becoming an integral part of our language.

This book provides many hours of entertainment, wherever you are. I see it as a worthy acknowledgement of the roles cats play in our lives – and in memory of my own family cats Achilles, Tabitha, Mary, Nelson, Othello, Perdita, Beau, Tarzan, Bill and Barney.

Patricia King

ABOUT THE PUZZLES

These varied and mind-questioning puzzles encompass several types. Many are word puzzles, some are a mixture of letters and known as 'jumbleys', while others include 'spidermite crosswords'. Here is an insight into the range of puzzles you will find in this book.

✤ SPIDERMITE CROSSWORDS Form simple frameworks using the words listed.

✤ WORDSEARCH PUZZLES Spotting words in a seemingly random medley of letters can stretch the mind.

✤ SPOT THE DIFFERENCE Fun pages where you are asked to find the difference between two pictures.

✤ JUMBLEYS Mixtures of letters that can be reassembled to form well-known words associated with cats.

✤ REBUS PUZZLES These puzzles are formed of letters and pictures which together make up words associated with cats.

✤ PAIRING UP Matching names to form a 'pairing-up' puzzle.

✤ POTPOURRI PUZZLES Wide and varied, but they all reveal fascinating facts about cats and how they have become integrated into our lives.

❧ CATS IN LITERATURE Poetry and verse are steeped in references to cats and you will no doubt remember many of them.

❧ QUOTATIONS AND PROVERBS These have always been popular and many help us to see how cats are interwoven with our lives.

The answers to these challenging puzzles are to be found at the end of this book.

I

PAIRING UP

Can you link up the following well-known people with their beloved cats?

Marilyn Monroe	Minou
Iris Murdoch	Mitsou
Florence Nightingale	Grimalkin
Nostradamus	General Butchkin
George Sand	Mr Bismarck

2

INSPIRATIONAL JUMBLEY

Can you decipher the name of T. S. Eliot's cat that inspired him to write *Old Possum's Book of Practical Cats*, which later led to the musical *Cats*?

ROLEJULMLY

3

DOMESTICATED CATS

How long ago is it estimated that cats began to be domesticated?

❧ 3,000 years
❧ 5,000 years
❧ 7,000 years
❧ 9,000 years
❧ 11,000 years

4

BREED PUZZLE

Which breed of cat was originated in the 1960s by the Californian cat breeder Ann Baker?

❧ Balinese
❧ Korat
❧ Ragdoll
❧ Spotted Mist
❧ Tiffanie

5

REMARKABLE VISION

Humans have peripheral vision of less than 180 degrees. How many degrees does a cat's vision encompass?

     ❧ 200 degrees
     ❧ 220 degrees
     ❧ 250 degrees
     ❧ 270 degrees
     ❧ 285 degrees

6

BRAIN CAPACITY

What proportion of a cat's weight does its brain constitute?

     ❧ 1 per cent
     ❧ 2 per cent
     ❧ 3 per cent
     ❧ 4 per cent
     ❧ 5 per cent

7

ANCESTRY

It is claimed that all cats originated from a common ancestor in South East Asia. How many years ago?

✿ Six million
✿ Eight million
✿ Ten million
✿ Eleven million
✿ Twelve million

8

AVERTING DANGER

If a black cat crosses your path, how many steps back should you take to avert bad luck?

✿ Three
✿ Six
✿ Nine
✿ Twelve
✿ Fifteen

CAT EQUIPMENT WORDSEARCH

P	E	T	I	N	N	S	U	P	A	L	F	T	A	C
N	E	U	T	K	E	E	T	S	T	B	O	W	G	O
C	A	T	F	I	D	D	U	T	E	R	I	N	N	L
O	A	L	I	T	T	E	R	T	R	A	Y	B	I	L
G	R	O	O	N	I	N	G	S	E	K	E	T	M	A
P	E	T	E	K	S	A	B	S	T	R	S	T	O	P
S	L	O	W	P	U	U	S	S	T	R	I	N	O	R
C	W	P	B	O	W	C	R	A	R	U	V	N	R	Y
R	O	O	M	I	O	W	L	A	T	W	O	R	G	S
Y	B	L	S	T	R	I	N	G	N	E	U	T	E	H
A	E	T	L	V	M	I	C	R	O	C	H	I	P	I
R	O	U	N	A	E	E	R	S	U	O	E	S	E	P
P	L	I	C	E	R	S	E	U	T	E	R	I	N	D
S	F	L	E	A	S	P	R	A	Y	M	I	C	R	O
I	D	E	N	T	I	T	Y	D	I	S	C	X	Y	G

Several pieces of equipment are needed when looking after a cat, as well as techniques and health considerations. Here are twelve that can be found in this puzzle – can you spot them?

- Basket
- Bowl
- Cat flap
- Collar
- Flea spray
- Grooming

- Identity disc
- Litter tray
- Microchip
- Neutering
- Pet insurance
- Wormers

IO

SACRED FELINE

Which cat breed, originating in Burma, is said to be a sacred temple cat?

♣ Birman
♣ Burmese
♣ Khmer
♣ Korat
♣ Siamese

II

STEPPE JUMBLEY

There are many different breeds of cat. Which popular one is mixed up here?

RISSANU LUBE

12

FELINE PULSE RATE

The human pulse rate is about half that of a cat when at rest.
What is a cat's normal range in beats per minute?

❧ 90 to 110
❧ 110 to 140
❧ 140 to 150
❧ 150 to 160

13

SAFER DRIVING

When were 'cat's eyes' first installed in British roads as a way to
make driving safer?

❧ 1920
❧ 1925
❧ 1930
❧ 1933
❧ 1937

14

IMPRESSIVE ATHLETE

Cats are famed for their skills at jumping. How many times greater than its own body height can a cat jump?

♣ Four
♣ Five
♣ Six
♣ Seven
♣ Eight

15

ROCK JUMBLEY

Delilah was the name of a favourite cat belonging to a 'rock legend' – his group of musicians immortalised her in a song of the same name. Can you decipher the name of Delilah's owner?

FRIEDED RUMCREY

POPULAR NURSERY RHYME

The earliest record of this rhyme's publication is said to be in *Songs for the Nursery*, printed in London in 1805.

However, it originated in Tudor times, during the reign of Queen Elizabeth I, from 1558 to 1603. It is claimed that one of her waiting ladies had an old cat which roamed throughout Windsor Castle and happened to walk under her throne. Its tail brushed against the queen's foot, startling her. Fortunately, this amused the queen, who gave the cat permission to wander about the throne-room on condition it kept it free from mice.

Can you complete this popular nursery rhyme:

> *Pussycat, pussycat, where have you been?*
> *I've been to London to visit the Queen,*
> *Pussycat, pussycat, what did you there,*
> *I...*

17

FRENCH CONNECTION

Which Queen of France kept Angora cats? Their descendants were taken to North America, where they became the originators of the Maine Coon breed.

- ♣ Adelaide of Aquitaine
- ♣ Anne of Austria
- ♣ Catherine de Medici
- ♣ Constance of Arles
- ♣ Marie Antoinette
- ♣ Maria Theresa of Austria

18

CAT-FISH JUMBLEY

Can you decipher from the jumbled letters below the name of a famous Russian composer and chemist who had a cat called Ryborov that learned to fish in winter through holes in the ice?

AXALEREND DOORBIN

TONGUE-TESTING JUMBLEY

From these jumbled letters, can you find the famous North American writer who liked to give his cats names such as Apollinaris, Zoroaster, Blatherskite and Sour Mash?

KARM WINTA

20

PRIVILEGED GIFT

Which famous screen idol was given a Siamese cat called Marcus by the legendary British actress Elizabeth Taylor?

- ♣ Richard Burton
- ♣ Gary Cooper
- ♣ James Dean
- ♣ Clint Eastwood
- ♣ Cary Grant
- ♣ Rock Hudson

SPOT THE DIFFERENCE

Lewis Carroll (Charles Lutwidge Dodgson, 1832–1898) wrote a whimsical story about a little girl (Alice) who falls down a rabbit hole into a strange country, where everything happens with fantastic illogicality.

In *Alice's Adventures in Wonderland*, Alice meets the Cheshire Cat, which slowly disappears until its smile is the last feature to go.

On the left is a reproduction of an illustration from this story. Can you spot ten differences in the version shown below?

CLASSIC ANIMATION

Which streetwise cat, created by the American team William Hanna and Joseph Barbera and led a gang of cats in a city?

- ♣ Cursed Cur
- ♣ Mr Big
- ♣ Tiger Cat
- ♣ Tim the Top
- ♣ Top Cat

23

TOURIST TROPHY CAT

Can you name the domestic breed of cat with a naturally occurring mutation that shortens its tail (some are tailless) in this jumbley? It is named after a self-governing British Crown Dependency island.

NAXM ACT

TREASURED COMPANION

A famous English author, who was fond of birds, initially refused to have cats until his daughter gave him one called William, renamed Williamina when she produced a litter. One kitten, white and deaf, became his constant companion. Who was the author?

❧ Charles Dickens
❧ Henry Fielding
❧ William Makepeace Thackeray
❧ Anthony Trollope

25

SOCIAL SKILLS

Which member of the cat family is the only one to live in a social group?

❧ Bengal Tiger
❧ Iberian Lynx
❧ Lion
❧ Mountain Cat

26

TREASURED TOM

Before World War Two (1939–1945) the British Civil Service employed a cat to control the rodent population. It was paid 2d a day by the Treasury. What was its name?

    ❧ Captain
    ❧ General
    ❧ Mr Jim
    ❧ Mouser
    ❧ Rufus
    ❧ Sid

27

ALLOWANCE JUMBLEY

In addition to the Treasury, which other British government agency employed cats, even granting them an official subsistence allowance?

STOP COFIEF

28

WITCH FAMILIAR

The name of the black American Shorthair cat that lives with Sabrina, the teenage witch (of comic book and TV series fame), can be found in this jumbley.

MALES ABREENGASH

29

BIG CAT

Which is the biggest of the 'big' cats, with an adult male weighing about 380 kg (840 lb)?

❧ African Lion
❧ Cheetah
❧ Jaguar
❧ Panther
❧ Siberian Tiger
❧ Snow Leopard

NORDIC LEGEND

In Scandinavian mythology, whose chariot was pulled along by black cats?

❧ Freya
❧ Heimdallr
❧ Nanna
❧ Saga
❧ Thor
❧ Vor

ELECTRICAL GENIUS

Nikola Tesla (1856–1943), the Serbian-American inventor, had a cat whose coat became charged with static electricity during a thunderstorm. Tesla investigated the phenomenon, and this research led to many scientific discoveries, including wireless communication. Can you decipher his cat's name?

ACKEM

COMIC CHARACTER

What is the name of the cat in the long-running animated television series *The Simpsons*?

☘ Clarence
☘ Duff
☘ Raindrop
☘ Santa's Little Helper
☘ Snowball
☘ Sunshine

FELINE CRITIC

Which world-famous crime author had a cat called Taki, his 'feline secretary', to which he read first drafts of his work?

☘ Eric Ambler
☘ Isaac Asimov
☘ Raymond Chandler
☘ G. K. Chesterton
☘ John Creasey

CAT BREEDS SPIDERMITE CROSSWORD

The range of cat breeds is extensive, with some well known for many years. Below are listed twenty breeds; how many of them can you fit into the spidermite crossword on the opposite page?

- ♣ Abyssinian
- ♣ American Short-hair
- ♣ Angora
- ♣ Balinese
- ♣ Birman
- ♣ Bobtail
- ♣ British Short-hair
- ♣ Burmese
- ♣ Chartreux
- ♣ Chinchilla

- ♣ Cornish Rex
- ♣ Foreign Lilac
- ♣ Havana Brown
- ♣ Himalayan
- ♣ Korat
- ♣ Manx
- ♣ Nebelung
- ♣ Russian Blue
- ♣ Scottish Fold
- ♣ Siamese

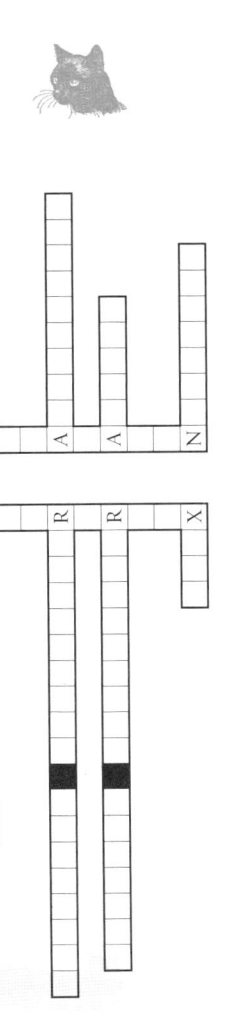

35

CHARTWELL FAVOURITE

Sir Winston Churchill's favourite cat was kept at Chartwell, his Kent home. What was its name?

⚜ Alfred the Great
⚜ Jock
⚜ Monty
⚜ Nelson
⚜ Patton
⚜ Tiger

36

MISSION IMPOSSIBLE?

Which Aesop fable demonstrated the moral 'It is easy to propose impossible remedies'?

⚜ *Belling the Cat*
⚜ *The Easy Time Cat*
⚜ *The Feline Friend*
⚜ *The Fraudulent Feline*
⚜ *Too Many Purrs*

37

TRAGIC END

Horace Walpole (1717–1797), the son of Robert Walpole (considered to be the first Prime Minister of England) had a cat named Selima, which unexpectedly died, but how?

- Drowned in a goldfish bowl
- Eaten by a crocodile
- Fell down a well
- Kicked in the head by a horse
- Run over by a landau
- Shot in an archery contest

38

REVENGE ATTACK?

The world-famous Scottish novelist and poet Sir Walter Scott (1771–1832) had a cat that regularly attacked his hunting dogs – until one killed him. Can you decipher his name from this jumbley?

SHINE

39

HEART BREAKING

When a family rift occurred over the burial of a famous author, a compromise was reached whereby the heart would be interred in a local churchyard and the body cremated, with the ashes taken to Westminster Abbey. However, after the heart was removed a calamity occurred – the household cat ate it. Whose heart was it?

HASMOT DRAHY

40

EUROPEAN LEGACY

Who introduced cats, as well as chickens, to Britain?

- ♣ The Jutes
- ♣ The Normans
- ♣ The Romans
- ♣ The Vikings

41

PAIRING UP

The cat family has evolved in many parts of the world. Here are some small wild cats that evolved in the Americas. Can you pair up their scientific and common names?

Common Name	Scientific Name
Bobcat	*Felis concolor*
Canada Lynx	*Felis colocolo*
Mountain Cat	*Felis pardalis*
Ocelot	*Felis lynx rufus*
Pampas Cat	*Felis jacobita*
Puma	*Felis lynx canadensis*

42

RARE BREED JUMBLEY

Can you decipher this breed from Indo-China in this jumbley?

MEKHR

43

PAIRING UP

The cat family has evolved in many parts of the world. Here are some small cats that evolved in Africa and Europe. Can you pair up their scientific and common names?

Fishing Cat	*Felis serval*
Iberian Lynx	*Felis margarita*
Marbled Cat	*Felis manul*
Pallas' Cat	*Felis lynx pardina*
Sand Cat	*Felis prionailurus viverrinus*
Serval	*Felis pardofelis marmorata*

44

SHORT-HAIRED CAT JUMBLEY

Can you detect the name of a popular cat in this jumbley?

SINABYSIAN

45

SAYING HELLO

Which famous British novelist, poet and critic wrote the following poem about his cat, Sarah Snow?

> *I was impressed to hear her say 'Hello'*
> *Not like a person, true*
> *It might not sound quite right to you*
> *More of a simple squeak or squawk —*
> *Still, that's what happens when cats talk.*

As a further clue, his novel *Lucky Jim* (published in 1954) reflected the flavour of Britain in the 1950s and was eventually translated into twenty languages.

- ♣ Kingsley Amis
- ♣ John Braine
- ♣ Lewis Carroll
- ♣ Philip Larkin
- ♣ Laurie Lee
- ♣ John Osborne

46

FABLE REBUS

Which Aesop fable demonstrated the moral 'It is easier to get into the enemy's toils than out again'?

AND THE
BEASTS

47

WITH MENACES!

What is the name of Dennis the Menace's cat – so called because of his mustard-coloured coat?

♣ Burger Bite
♣ English Mustard
♣ French Mustard
♣ Hot Dog
♣ Mustard
♣ Pot Roast

48

FELINE WISDOM

Who said the following? 'Cats are smarter than dogs. You can't get eight cats to pull a sled through snow.'

- ❧ Ken Anderson
- ❧ Caspar Badrutt
- ❧ John Baker
- ❧ Ralph Fiennes
- ❧ Jeff Valdez

49

MAGNETIC FORCE

Which plant is said to be irresistible to cats?

- ❧ Catmint
- ❧ Cattail
- ❧ Clover
- ❧ Common Catsear
- ❧ Moth Mullein
- ❧ Mouse-ear Hawkweed

SHORT-HAIRED BREEDS
WORDSEARCH

E	S	C	O	T	T	I	S	H	F	O	L	D	A	C
S	U	P	A	R	A	N	A	A	O	C	T	I	C	O
E	X	R	S	Y	R	I	A	V	O	L	R	I	C	R
L	O	U	I	S	E	J	W	A	K	W	X	I	T	N
K	A	S	N	T	S	W	O	N	P	I	C	N	R	I
I	O	S	G	T	E	X	N	A	T	A	Y	C	A	S
R	U	I	A	N	M	E	S	E	T	I	R	A	S	H
K	I	N	P	U	R	R	E	A	M	I	E	R	N	R
R	E	M	U	R	U	S	S	I	A	N	B	L	U	E
E	B	I	R	M	B	A	I	L	L	S	I	U	I	X
X	A	M	A	E	J	E	A	P	A	I	R	A	N	D
N	M	A	N	K	O	R	M	T	Y	R	L	A	Y	A
A	N	G	O	R	O	B	E	N	A	M	M	P	O	V
W	A	R	X	N	A	R	S	I	N	A	P	U	R	A
L	I	A	T	B	O	B	E	S	E	N	A	P	A	J

Many short-haired breeds have been domesticated and kept as pets. Here, fourteen of them can be found in this wordsearch – can you spot them?

- Bengal
- Burmese
- Cornish Rex
- Havana
- Japanese Bobtail
- Korat
- Malayan

- Manx
- Ocicat
- Russian Blue
- Scottish Fold
- Selkirk Rex
- Siamese
- Singapura

51

A PASSING OMEN

In the Channel Island of Guernsey, it was said that to see a black cat passing a window is a sign that...

❧ A stranger is coming
❧ You are about to meet a lover
❧ An aged relative will appear
❧ Bad luck is coming
❧ Good luck is coming
❧ A storm is brewing

52

DEATH PENALTY JUMBLEY

In Egypt, severe punishments were associated with a goddess often depicted as a woman with the head of a cat and given to anyone killing a cat. Can you spot the name of the goddess in this jumbley?

ATBEST

53

PAIRING UP

Cats of different colours have been seen as omens of certain outcomes, depending on the country. Can you match these up?

Black cat (Britain)	Bad luck
Black cat (North America)	Good luck
Black-white-grey mixture	Bad luck
Stray tortoiseshell cat	Good luck
White cat (most countries)	Misfortune

54

CAT ADAGE

If someone is said to be slovenly, uncouth or unkempt in appearance, what are they described as?

Like something the...

55

FELINE PLAY

Which play by the North American playwright Tennessee Williams (1911–1983) won the Pulitzer Prize for Drama in 1955? It was later made into a film starring Elizabeth Taylor and Paul Newman, and has the word 'cat' in its title.

56

CAT-LAP

This colloquial and contemptuous term was widely used in the 1700s. What did it refer to?

- ❧ Gin and water mixture
- ❧ Ginger beer
- ❧ Sour beer
- ❧ Tea or other non-alcoholic drinks
- ❧ Watered-down whiskey
- ❧ Watery gruel

57

GUNMEN BEWARE

Which popular spoof western film appeared in 1965, starring
Jane Fonda, Lee Marvin and Michael Callan?

    ❧ *Cat Ballou*
    ❧ *Cat Capers*
    ❧ *Feline Follies*
    ❧ *Nine Lives at Noon*
    ❧ *Tom Cat Frolics*

58

CAT MARKET

During the nineteenth and twentieth centuries, 'cat market'
became a popular term – but for what?

    ❧ A country prison
    ❧ Many people speaking at the same time
    ❧ A market bursting with vibrancy and work
    ❧ A nefarious group of people
    ❧ A place to buy a cat
    ❧ A recruitment office for the army

59

FELINE DEFENCE LEAGUE

Which famous writer's cat, Mysouff, would accompany him from his house and then go to meet him on his return? This writer founded the Feline Defence League.

- ❧ Honoré de Balzac
- ❧ Charles Dickens
- ❧ Alexandre Dumas
- ❧ Franz Kafka
- ❧ Anthony Trollope
- ❧ H. G. Wells

60

EARLY DAYS

In which region are cats said to have been first domesticated?

- ❧ Egypt
- ❧ Lebanon
- ❧ Northern Morocco
- ❧ Palestine
- ❧ Southern Cyprus

DOUBLE TOP

Which of Queen Victoria's favourite cats survived her to be inherited by her son Edward VII – making it a cat that was owned by two monarchs?

❖ Black Beauty
❖ Highland Lass
❖ Laurel
❖ Othello
❖ Perdita
❖ White Heather

DARK INSIGHT

Whose cat, Beppo, apparently drank milk from a skull and 'helped' to write many of his owner's poems?

❖ William Blake
❖ Robert Burns
❖ Lord Byron
❖ Percy Bysshe Shelley

63

LEGENDARY LEADER

What was the name of the cat that accompanied Sir Ernest Shackleton's *Endurance* expedition, during which his ship was crushed by ice?

✤ Barney
✤ Dove Tail
✤ Mrs Chippy
✤ Polar
✤ Scramble
✤ Southern Hero

64

IN THE BLOOD?

Which Aesop fable demonstrated the moral 'Nature will out', to be found in this jumbley?

ETH ACT DEANIM

65

NOT A FAREWELL

Which author was renowned for his love of cats, especially polydactyl (six-toed) ones? Some of them still live in his house, now a museum, in Florida.

♣ William Faulkner
♣ Ernest Hemingway
♣ Henry James
♣ John Steinbeck
♣ P. G. Wodehouse

66

CAT THAT GOT THE CREAM

Which Shakespearean character said: 'I am as vigilant as a cat to steal cream'?

♣ Cassio in *Othello*
♣ Falstaff in *Henry IV Part I*
♣ Orlando in *As You Like It*
♣ Puck in *A Midsummer Night's Dream*
♣ Shylock in *The Merchant of Venice*

SPOT THE DIFFERENCE

In Norse mythology, cats were associated with storms and dogs with wind, with the phrase 'To rain cats and dogs' dating from at least the mid-seventeenth century.

This illustration by Theodor Seuss Geisel (Dr Seuss, 1904–1991), an American writer, poet and cartoonist widely known for his children's books, shows people carefully avoiding cats and dogs which continue to fall from the sky.

On the left is a reproduction of one of his cartoons; can you spot ten differences in the version shown below?

68

COLOUR REBUS

Can you spot a colour variation in a cat breed in this picture and word puzzle?

 PATTERN

69

FIRST KITTENS

Which United States president rescued three half-frozen kittens and took them to the White House, where they joined Tabby, who was the earliest recorded feline of that residence?

- ♣ Ulysses S. Grant
- ♣ Andrew Johnson
- ♣ Abraham Lincoln
- ♣ Franklin Pierce
- ♣ George Washington

70

CATWOMAN JUMBLEY

In 1967, this famous American actress and singer was the third woman to play Catwoman. Can you see her name in this puzzle?

HTAREA TIKT

71

HIGH FLYER

What was the name of Charles Lindbergh's black cat, which accompanied him on many of his flights?

- ♣ Birdie
- ♣ Florence
- ♣ Flossy
- ♣ Maisie
- ♣ Patsy
- ♣ Trudy

72

MORE THAN A LODGER

Who wrote 'When a cat adopts you there is nothing to be done about it except to put up with it until the wind changes'?

❧ T. S. Eliot
❧ Stephen King
❧ Milan Kundera
❧ Beatrix Potter
❧ Nigel Slater

73

ORDER, ORDER!

Whose cat would stalk out of a room, protesting loudly, if a guest talked too long or loudly?

❧ Clement Attlee
❧ William Gladstone
❧ D. H. Lawrence
❧ Jean-Paul Sartre
❧ H. G. Wells

74

FISHY NATURE

Which 1935 American folk opera by George Gershwin, with lyrics by Ira Gershwin and DuBose Heyward, had a road known as Catfish Row?

  ❧ *An American in Paris*
  ❧ *Funny Face*
  ❧ *Lady, Be Good*
  ❧ *Porgy and Bess*
  ❧ *Strike Up the Band*

75

LITERARY MERCENARY

In which of Frederick Forsyth's novels does the character Cat Shannon appear?

  ❧ *The Day of the Jackal*
  ❧ *The Dogs of War*
  ❧ *The Fourth Protocol*
  ❧ *The Odessa File*
  ❧ *The Shepherd*

ROMAN REBUS

Which Roman statesman, who became consul in 195 BC, can you decipher in this puzzle?

O

77

GUT WRENCHING!

What is the name of a type of cord prepared from natural fibres found in the walls of animal intestines, usually from sheep and goats? It was widely used as strings for musical instruments.

78

THEATRICAL DISPLEASURE

People displeased with a theatrical performance have been known to make these. Can you name them?

❧ Catcalls
❧ Catcrows
❧ Catshouts
❧ Catyells

79

BURNING DESIRE

In which of William Shakespeare's plays does the following appear: 'The cat, with eyne of burning coal, Now couches fore the mouse's hole'?

❧ *As You Like It*
❧ *Hamlet*
❧ *Much Ado About Nothing*
❧ *Pericles, Prince of Tyre*
❧ *The Tempest*

LONG-HAIRED BREEDS
WORDSEARCH

E	S	E	N	A	V	A	J	A	P	A	N	N	E	S
C	I	C	A	N	S	I	A	M	E	H	A	V	A	T
A	B	E	R	G	U	C	Y	M	R	M	I	C	A	E
T	E	S	I	O	A	Y	B	U	R	A	G	D	O	I
H	R	A	G	R	J	M	A	I	N	E	C	O	O	N
O	I	Y	O	Y	L	R	B	A	L	I	N	E	S	A
U	A	G	R	L	X	I	S	L	T	A	N	A	P	F
S	N	O	A	D	C	C	O	Y	I	A	M	I	E	F
A	F	M	R	I	C	D	M	E	F	T	H	O	R	I
N	O	R	W	E	G	I	A	N	F	O	R	E	S	T
S	R	O	R	A	B	A	L	I	A	E	S	E	I	R
E	E	R	R	A	N	E	E	S	E	N	I	L	A	B
T	S	T	I	R	A	M	E	N	N	I	C	A	N	E
E	T	A	H	K	W	B	P	A	I	R	T	H	Q	U
A	M	E	R	I	C	A	N	C	U	R	L	T	U	A

Long-haired breeds are claimed to be the quietest and least active of cat breeds. Thirteen of them can be found in this wordsearch – can you spot them?

- American Curl
- Angora
- Balinese
- Birman
- Cymric
- Javanese
- Maine Coon
- Norwegian Forest
- Persian
- Ragdoll
- Siberian Forest
- Somali
- Tiffanie

81

MODEL PARADE

Where do fashion models parade themselves to display their clothes? You might also see it on the bridge of a ship. Is it:

- ❧ Catplank
- ❧ Catrun
- ❧ Catstroll
- ❧ Catwalk
- ❧ Catway

82

SOUND ONLY

Early radio enthusiasts might have heard of a term usually associated with crystal sets. What is it?

- ❧ Cat's ear
- ❧ Cat's paw
- ❧ Cat's tongue
- ❧ Cat's whisker
- ❧ Cat's whistle

83

CATS' PLEDGE

Where in North America is there still a statute forbidding the supply of beer to cats?

- ♣ Albuquerque, New Mexico
- ♣ Charleston, South Carolina
- ♣ Milwaukee, Wisconsin
- ♣ Natchez, Mississippi
- ♣ Springfield, Tennessee
- ♣ Wichita, Kansas

84

FELINE COMPANY

A general who fought in the American Civil War loved cats so much that during his campaigns in the Mexican-American War he wrote to his daughter asking for a kitten to be sent to him. Can you see his name in this jumbley?

TROBER E. ELE

85

PAIRING UP

Cats are steeped in omens – some good, others bad. Here is a medley of them. How many can you match up?

Cat continuously sneezes	Visiting clergyman
Cat cries as you leave home	Storm to come
Cat licks its tail	Change in the weather
Cat sneezes once	Unlucky
Cat sneezes thrice	Lucky for the household
Cat with its back to a fire	Expect a light shower
Cat washing in a doorway	Indicates rain
Cat scratches a table leg	Long, wet period
Cat washes its face and ears	Everyone catches a cold

86

LORD MAYOR'S CAT

Which Lord Mayor of London had a famous cat?

- ❧ John de Gisors
- ❧ John Humphrey
- ❧ Boris Johnson
- ❧ Paul Mesurier
- ❧ John Tate
- ❧ Dick Whittington

87

HOME FROM HOME

Who was so devoted to his cat, Foss, that when he moved house he had a new one built exactly like the old one so that Foss would feel at home?

- ❧ Arnold Bennett
- ❧ John Bunyan
- ❧ Wilkie Collins
- ❧ Bernard Cornwell
- ❧ Edward Lear

88

WATERY REBUS

There is a small wild cat that has slightly webbed toes and lives in mangrove swamps in China, India, Myanmar and Sri Lanka. Can you spot it in this puzzle? The illustration is by the American cartoonist George Herriman (1880–1944), best known for his comic strip *Krazy Kat*.

ITALIAN FREEDOM

In ancient Rome the cat was a symbol of freedom. The goddess of Liberty was usually represented together with a cat, but how was the cat depicted?

♣ At her feet
♣ In her arms
♣ On her lap
♣ Perched on her head
♣ Sitting on her shoulder

QUESTIONABLE MORAL FIBRE?

Which Shakespearean character is accused of cowardice in the following words?

> ... *live a coward in thine own esteem,*
> *Letting 'I dare not' wait upon 'I would',*
> *Like the poor cat 'i' the adage?*

♣ The Fool in *King Lear*
♣ Macbeth (by his wife) in *Macbeth*
♣ Petruchio in *The Taming of the Shrew*
♣ Sir Andrew Aguecheek in *Twelfth Night*

EQUITABLE EXISTENCE

If a man and a woman lead a 'cat and dog life', which of the
following describes them?

      🍀 Always quarrelling and snapping
      🍀 Cuddling together in bed
      🍀 Eating from the same bowl
      🍀 Ignoring each other
      🍀 Respecting each other's nature
      🍀 Ridden with fleas

92

FELINE FLIGHT

Guy Gibson VC, the famous bomber pilot in World War Two (1939–1945), had a cat that accompanied him on many missions. What was her name?

- ❧ Flight
- ❧ Storm
- ❧ Sunshine
- ❧ Windy

93

REBUS FABLE

Which Aesop fable demonstrates the moral 'Better one safe way than a hundred on which you cannot reckon'?

94

RELIGIOUS LOVE

When preaching, the Prophet Muhammad would hold his favourite cat in his arms. Because of his love of cats, they are free to enter mosques, with Islamic Law forbidding killing them. Can you decipher this treasured cat's name?

AZUMEZ

95

GOING FOR A DIP

Which cat is also known as the 'Swimming Cat'?

- ❧ Abyssinian
- ❧ American Curl
- ❧ Balinese
- ❧ Havana Brown
- ❧ Maine Coon
- ❧ Turkish Van

SPOT THE DIFFERENCE

This illustration is from *The Book of Fairy Tales*, published in 1914 and illustrated by Henry Matthew Brock (1875–1960), the well-known British illustrator and landscape painter.

The illustration depicts a sneaky cat stealing a person's clothing while they bathe in a river. Can you detect the ten differences from the illustration on the left to the one on the right?

97

DOG ASSOCIATION

Which cat breed, originated in Great Britain in 1960, is nicknamed 'Poodle Cat'?

- ♣ Cornish Rex
- ♣ Devon Rex
- ♣ Manx
- ♣ Munchkin
- ♣ Ragdoll
- ♣ Tiffanie

98

TALKATIVE JUMBLEY

A story by Saki (the famed Scottish writer Hector Hugh Munro) tells of a cat that learns to talk, causing great consternation among his owner's guests, who realise the indiscretions he may have witnessed. What is the cat's name?

MORETOBRY

99

POLITICAL LEADERS

On the death of Screaming Lord Sutch in 1999, The Official Monster Raving Loony Party elected joint leaders – Alan 'Howling Laud' Hope and his cat. A proposed law was that no other cat shall be given the same name as Hope's cat. Can you spot the name in this puzzle?

DU

100

SENSITIVE DESCRIPTION

In 1902, who wrote a wonderfully accurate description of a cat's nature in his story *The Cat that Walked by Himself*?

❧ Lewis Carroll
❧ T. S. Eliot
❧ Rudyard Kipling
❧ Edward Lear

101

HYBRID JUMBLEY

Can you see the name of a cat breed that is a hybrid between a Burmese and a Siamese in this jumbley?

NEOSETNIK

102

TOUCH OF GINGER

Kathleen Hale (1898–2000), British author, illustrator and artist, wrote a number of well-known books on the experiences of a marmalade cat. What was his name?

- ❧ Dizzy
- ❧ Jasper
- ❧ Lysander
- ❧ Marmaduke
- ❧ Oberon
- ❧ Orlando

103

UPDATED NURSERY RHYME

This rhyme dates from the sixteenth century, and originally the cat drowned. Later versions had the cat being rescued to teach children not to harm animals. Can you add the last line to this rhyme?

Ding dong bell,
Pussy's in the well,
Who put her in?
Little Johnny Flynn,
Who pulled her out?

...

104

EARLY TAMING

Which was the first cat species to be tamed? Can you spot it in this jumbley?

FANARIC DATCLIW

WILD CATS
SPIDERMITE CROSSWORD

The range of wild cats is extensive, from large ones such as lions and tigers to smaller, although no less important, ones in the Americas, Africa and Eurasia. Here are eighteen of them; which ones can you fit into the spidermite on the opposite page? We have added eight key letters to help you.

- ❦ Asian Golden
- ❦ Black-footed
- ❦ Bobcat
- ❦ Caracal
- ❦ Cheetah
- ❦ Clouded Leopard
- ❦ Jaguar
- ❦ Jaguarundi
- ❦ Kodkod

- ❦ Leopard
- ❦ Lynx
- ❦ Ocelot
- ❦ Pampas
- ❦ Puma
- ❦ Rusty Spotted Cat
- ❦ Scottish
- ❦ Spanish
- ❦ Tiger

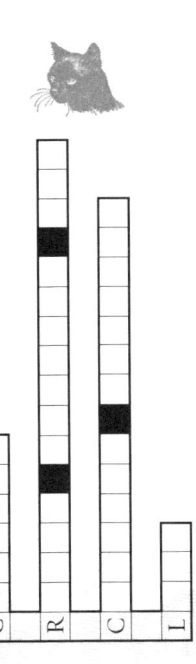

106

NAVAL CAT

In 1949 a British frigate came under fire from Chinese communist gun batteries in what became known as the Yangtze Incident. Many crew members were killed or wounded, including the ship's cat. Later, a film was made of the event, in which the frigate was brought out of retirement to play herself. Can you find her name in this jumbley?

HMS SHAMETTY

107

EAR JUMBLEY

Which breed with folded ears can you see in this jumbley?

SHOSTICT DOLF

108

SHIP'S CAT HONOURED

The wounded ship's cat in puzzle 106 was successfully treated and brought back to England, where he was awarded the campaign medal. He was also awarded the Dickin Medal, the only cat to ever receive this, and the Blue Cross Medal. On his death, he was buried with full naval orders and his grave is in the People's Dispensary for Sick Animal's Ilford Animal Cemetery. What was this brave cat's name?

BEAL AMANSE NIMOS

109

STUMPY TAIL JUMBLEY

Which oriental breed has a short tail?

SPANAJEE TOILBAB

110

WILD CAT PUZZLE

One small wild cat, native to an area from Saharan Africa to Asia, has thick hair between pads on its feet and obtains most of its water requirements from desert rodents. Can you find it in this picture puzzle?

111

NO PLACE LIKE HOME

Who said the following?

A home without a cat, and a well-fed, well-petted and properly revered cat, may be a perfect home, perhaps, but how can it prove its title?

🐾 Louisa May Alcott
🐾 Thomas Ashe
🐾 Daniel Denton
🐾 William Penn
🐾 Mark Twain

112

PAIRING UP

Can you pair up these 'Ancients' with their views on cats?

Aesop (c.620—560 BC)	Clean (noting that unnatural odours could make them mad)
Pliny (AD 23—79)	Devious and cunning
Plutarch (AD c.46—120)	Associated with lust

113

HOMESPUN WISDOM

Can you complete the following Old English saying?

Honest as the cat when...

114

PAINFUL RESULT

Can you name the whip made of knotted thongs? The picture here is a clue.

115

CRAMPED STYLE

When a bosun punished an unlucky sailor with the whip featured in puzzle 114, he could not stand close to rigging, spars or men because the thongs might get caught. This gave rise to an often-used saying when space is restricted. Can you guess it?

♣ Get out of my way
♣ Give me space
♣ Let the cat see the dog
♣ No room to swing a cat
♣ Stand clear please

LITERARY JUMBLEY

What famous fairytale, originally written by Charles Perrault (1628–1703) and called *Le Maître Chat, ou Le Chat Botté*, carried the two important themes of work and *savoir faire*, and of dress, good looks and youth, to win the heart of a princess?

SUPS NI SOBOT

117

CAT CLOCK!

Which Shakespearean character said: 'Thrice the brinded cat hath mew'd'?

♣ First Witch in *Macbeth*
♣ Lady Macbeth in *Macbeth*
♣ Lady Macduff in *Macbeth*
♣ Viola in *Twelfth Night*

118

HEINOUS ACT

What did the Prisoners (Temporary Discharge for Ill Health) Act 1913 become known as? It legalised hunger strikes that many suffragettes underwent, and mandated them to be released when they became ill. The catch being that the police could re-imprison them as soon as they recovered.

- Cat and Mouse Act
- Sick as a Cat Act
- Fat Cat Act
- Cat and Dog Act

119

ROCKY SITUATION

Can you complete the following saying?

As nervous as a cat with a long tail...

120

MUSICAL FELINE

What was the name of the first studio album recorded by the American glam metal band Poison, released in 1986 through Enigma Records?

♣ *Look What the Cat Dragged In*
♣ *The Carpeted Cat*
♣ *The Cat-flap Cat*
♣ *The Scraggy Mog Tale*

121

PAIRING UP

Can you link these cats with the TV shows and animations in which they appeared?

Cat	*Star Trek: The Next Generation*
Chance (T-Bone)	*Red Dwarf*
Salem Saberhagen	*CatDog*
Spot	*SWAT Kats*
The Cat	*Sabrina, the Teenage Witch*

WILD CATS NATIVE TO AFRICA AND ASIA WORDSEARCH

B	C	H	E	E	T	A	H	X	L	A	V	R	E	S
A	O	O	X	L	P	U	R	A	A	X	M	I	R	N
R	I	R	N	T	H	E	L	W	C	E	L	L	M	O
D	X	J	U	N	G	L	E	C	A	T	M	N	O	W
F	I	S	H	I	N	G	C	A	R	T	W	E	L	L
I	S	O	T	O	P	C	R	A	A	S	T	I	M	E
S	O	L	E	O	P	A	R	D	C	A	R	A	C	O
H	O	L	P	I	T	A	X	N	Y	W	X	O	J	P
I	P	V	Z	D	A	N	L	M	T	Y	R	P	W	A
N	E	A	T	A	C	D	E	L	B	R	A	M	I	R
G	O	A	H	E	D	A	S	F	A	A	T	O	L	D
C	A	R	L	A	N	X	W	O	N	S	H	E	D	S
A	B	I	B	L	A	A	C	K	M	B	C	A	C	T
T	O	P	M	O	S	T	Q	U	O	T	I	A	A	N
N	B	O	R	N	E	A	N	B	A	Y	C	A	T	E

Many well-known wild cats are native to large areas of Africa and Asia. Fourteen of them can be found in this wordsearch – can you spot them?

- Bornean Bay Cat
- Caracal
- Cheetah
- Fishing Cat
- Jungle Cat
- Leopard
- Lion
- Marbled Cat
- Pallas' Cat
- Sand Cat
- Serval
- Snow Leopard
- Tiger
- Wildcat

123

LIMITATIONS

Which type of establishment in the tenth century was only allowed to keep cats, other animals being banned?

♣ Convent
♣ Dock warehouse
♣ Food storehouse
♣ Kings' residence
♣ Monastery

124

ALMOST DEITY

Can you complete the following anonymous quotation?

Thousands of years ago, cats were worshipped as Gods...

125

PAIRING UP

Can you link the following literary cats with their authors?

Bagheera	Dr Seuss (*The Cat in the Hat*)
Cheshire Cat	J. K. Rowling (Harry Potter books)
Crookshanks	Beatrix Potter
Smiley Cat	Lewis Carroll (*Alice in Wonderland*)
Tom Kitten	Rudyard Kipling (*The Jungle Book*)

126

JOYS OF LIFE

Albert Schweitzer (1875–1965), philosopher, physician and organist, said: 'There are two means of refuge from the miseries of life.' Can you name them?

127

PLUM PROBLEM

According to P. G. Wodehouse (known to his friends as Plum) the problem with cats is that they:

- ♣ Bring unwanted creatures (presents) into the house
- ♣ Destroy furniture
- ♣ Don't usually get along with dogs
- ♣ Have no tact
- ♣ Want praise

128

INEVITABLE OUTCOME

Can you complete the following quote by the American poet Ogden Nash (1902–1971), known for his light verse?

The trouble with a kitten is that eventually...

129

PAIRING UP

Can you link these famous cats with the book, film, play or show in which they appeared?

Eureka	*Austin Powers*
Figaro	*The Wizard of Oz*
Ginger	*Macbeth*
Graymalkin	*Pinocchio*
Kitty	*The Chronicles of Narnia*
Mr Bigglesworth	*Little House on the Prairie*

130

PLAYFUL NATURE

Can you complete this quote from Miguel de Cervantes (1547–1616), Spanish novelist, poet and playwright?

Those who'll play with cats...

131

EARLY HERO JUMBLEY

In 1854, famished British and French troops occupying Sevastopol were led by a cat to caches of food. The cat was adopted by soldiers and taken to England when troops returned. He was known by two names, one being Sevastopol Tom; what was the other?

MARCIEN OMT

132

CHILDREN'S LITERATURE

Eliza Lee Cabot Follen (1787–1860), American author and abolitionist, adapted an old English nursery rhyme. It began:

> *Three little kittens they lost their mittens*
> *And they began to cry,*
> *'Oh, mother dear, we sadly fear*
> *Our mittens we have lost.'*

What punishment did the mother decree?

133

ANIMAL EGALITARIANISM!

Can you fill in the gaps (all animal names) in this quotation by
Sir Winston Churchill?

> *I like pigs.*
> *... look up to us.*
> *... look down on us.*
> *... treat us as equals.*

134

ARTISTIC INSIGHT

Who said the following?

*God is really only another artist. He invented the giraffe, the elephant and the
cat. He has no real style. He just goes on trying other things.*

♣ Édouard Manet (1832–1883)
♣ Claude Monet (1840–1926)
♣ Pablo Picasso (1881–1973)
♣ Vincent van Gogh (1853–1890)

HIDDEN CREATIVITY

Who said the following?

No matter how much cats fight, there always seems to be plenty of kittens.

❦ Aphra Behn
❦ Sir Arthur Conan Doyle
❦ Abraham Lincoln
❦ Anna Sewell
❦ George Washington

IRISH INSPIRATION

Can you provide the next line in this poem about a cat by the Irish poet, dramatist and prose writer William Butler Yeats (1865–1939)?

Minnaloushe creeps through the grass,
Alone, important and wise,
And lifts to the changing moon...

137

CATS, GAMES AND COMICS

Can you link these cats to the video games and comics in which
they appeared?

Big	*Get Fuzzy*
Cait Smith	*Dilbert*
Catbert	*Sonic Adventure*
Chubby Huggs	*Final Fantasy VII*

138

PERCEPTIVE VIEWPOINT

Who said: 'The smallest feline is a masterpiece'?

♣ Caravaggio (1571–1610)
♣ Giovanni Boccaccio (1313–1375)
♣ Leonardo da Vinci (1452–1519)
♣ Michelangelo (1475–1564)

AMERICAN TWIST

The English dramatist and poet Ben Jonson (1572–1637), coined the term 'Care killed the cat' in *Every Man in His Humour* (1598). At that time, 'care' meant worry and sorrow.

William Shakespeare (1564–1616) performed in this play and, never averse to purloining a good line, a year later used it in *Much Ado About Nothing*.

'Care killed the cat' remained a popular saying until it was corrupted in an article in *The Galveston Daily News* in 1898. This is the oldest newspaper in Texas, now known as *The Daily News*.

Can you guess what this change was?

♣ Care sometimes kills
♣ Curiosity killed the cat
♣ Going feet up
♣ Killing fields
♣ Nosey cats beware
♣ Mind the cat's nose

FOLKLORE PUZZLE

Can you work out the saying hidden in the following puzzle?

141

WHO'S THE TOY?

Who said the following?

*When I play with my cat, who knows whether she is
not amusing herself with me more than I with her?*

♣ Thomas Aquinas (1225–1274)
♣ Michel de Montaigne (1533–1592)
♣ John Duns Scotus (1265–1308)
♣ Martinus Smiglecius (1564–1618)

LUNAR LUNACY

What did the cat do when the cow jumped over the moon in a famous Tudor nursery rhyme?

- ❧ Played the fiddle
- ❧ Laughed hysterically
- ❧ Rolled on its back
- ❧ Slinked away
- ❧ Went to sleep

143

LUCKY LEGACY

During the 1940s, a well-known cat was born and lived as a ship's cat, serving on Royal Navy aircraft carriers. He safely travelled over 30,000 miles during his naval service and some believe he is one reason why a black cat is considered lucky in Great Britain. What was his name?

- ♣ Blackie
- ♣ Fluffy
- ♣ Lucky
- ♣ Sailor
- ♣ Skipper
- ♣ Tiddles

144

FAMILY FORTUNES

In which Shakespearean play does the following quote appear?

*... my mother weeping, my father wailing, my sister crying,
our maid howling, our cat wringing her hands...*

❧ *As You Like It*
❧ *Much Ado About Nothing*
❧ *The Taming of the Shrew*
❧ *Twelfth Night*
❧ *Two Gentlemen of Verona*

145

SALTY ENDEAVOUR

Can you complete the following quote by the eminent
English philosopher, statesman and essayist Francis Bacon
(1561–1626)?

A cat will never drown if she...

WITCHES' CATS
SPIDERMITE CROSSWORD

Cats and witches are a well-known combination. Many of these cats have become popular through comics, films and legends. Here are eighteen of them; which ones can you fit into the spidermite on the opposite page? We have added eight key letters to help you.

❧ Annie

❧ Arbis

❧ Bewitched

❧ Charity

❧ Dreama

❧ Elphaba

❧ Glinda

❧ Hagatha

❧ Hermione

❧ Kira

❧ Mitzy

❧ Mrs Cantrip

❧ Rowena

❧ Sabrina

❧ Traci Thirteen

❧ Witch Hazel

❧ Xanadu

❧ Zelda

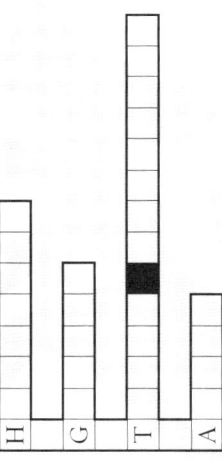

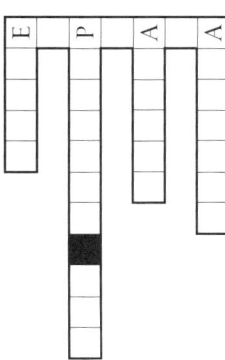

147

DIRE RESULTS

Can you find a popular saying in this picture?

148

RELIGIOUS INTOLERANCE

The god-like status of cats in many religions was eroded when Christianity spread across Europe, with its condemnation of false gods. Cats were considered manifestations of evil and many were killed, becoming almost extinct by 1400. However, when Europe became dominated by plague, this was a disaster – can you guess why?

❧ No cats to cuddle
❧ No cats to eat
❧ No cats to keep churches free from mice
❧ No cats to kill rats
❧ No cats to guard stored grain

149

MEDIEVAL SAYING

After selling a piglet and putting it in a sack, the seller often cunningly switched it for a cat; it was not until the buyer arrived home that the deception became apparent, when the...

- ♣ cat began to repeatedly squeal
- ♣ cat ran back to the stall holder
- ♣ cat was let out of the bag

150

BREED REBUS

Can you decipher this breed in the following puzzle? It has a silver-blue coat and a semi-cobby body and originated pre-1700s in Thailand.

KO

151

SNOOZE TIME

What is the cat-related term given to having a brief doze?

- 🐾 Catnap
- 🐾 Catnod
- 🐾 Catpeepybyes
- 🐾 Catsleep
- 🐾 Catsnooze

152

NEW FOR OLD

In 1760 a book entitled *The Life and Adventures of a Cat* was published anonymously and it quickly became popular. The hero's name was Tom the Cat and the name was soon applied to all male cats. How was a male cat referred to prior to this?

- 🐾 Buck
- 🐾 Bull
- 🐾 Cock
- 🐾 Jack
- 🐾 Ram

153

BREED REBUS

Can you name this cat with a jet-black coat that resembles patent leather? It originated in the 1960s in the USA.

 AY

154

DEADLY DEATH!

Charles I of England believed his black cat brought him good luck and had it carefully guarded. What happened the day after the cat died?

♣ Battle of Marston Moor – defeat
♣ Battle of Naseby – defeat
♣ Charles I's surrender to the Scots
♣ Charles I's trial began
♣ Charles I was arrested
♣ Charles I was executed

155

STROKE OF LUCK

One superstition thought to bring good luck was to stroke a black cat three times while reciting this rhyme:

Black cat, cross my path,
Good fortune bring to home and hearth,
When I am away from home,

Can you provide the last line?

156

NO SLOUCH!

The domestic cat can reach 30 mph (48 kph) when terrified and trying to escape. How fast do you think it can run in normal conditions?

♣ 15 mph (24 kph)
♣ 20 mph (32 kph)
♣ 25 mph (40 kph)

BASEBALL JUMBLEY

What is the name of the 1951 film, starring Jan Sterling, Ray Millard and Orangey the Cat, about a cat that inherits a Brooklyn baseball team and is a more successful manager (despite the players' objections) than most human team-owners? Can you spot it in this jumbley?

BURRABH

158

LUCKY FOLLOWING

According to superstition, if you meet a cat in the street and it follows you, what will happen to you?

- ❧ You will be adopted by the cat
- ❧ You will soon come into some money
- ❧ You will have a happy marriage
- ❧ You will get a tax rebate
- ❧ You will inherit a large estate

159

GRAVE SITUATION

According to superstition in Transylvania, what is the significance of a cat jumping over a grave?

- ♣ Cat becomes adopted by a witch
- ♣ Churchyard becomes cursed
- ♣ Corpse becomes a vampire
- ♣ Country is about to be invaded
- ♣ Infertility in the cat owner's family
- ♣ Onlookers become blind

160

CARTOON CAT DEBUT

When did *Sylvester the Cat* first appear in a cartoon? Was it:

- ♣ 1940
- ♣ 1942
- ♣ 1945
- ♣ 1947
- ♣ 1950
- ♣ 1955

161

TAKING YOUR TEMPERATURE

Which philosopher said: 'If a dog jumps onto your lap it is because he is fond of you, but if a cat does the same thing it is because your lap is warmer'?

- ♣ A. N. Whitehead (1861–1947)
- ♣ Bertrand Russell (1872–1970)
- ♣ Albert Einstein (1879–1955)

162

VANISHING CAT

Who wrote the following lines about a cat that was never there?

Macavity, Macavity, there's no one like Macavity,
There was never a Cat of such deceitfulness and suavity...

- ♣ T. S. Eliot (1888–1965)
- ♣ Thomas Gray (1716–1771)
- ♣ John Keats (1795–1821)
- ♣ Rudyard Kipling (1865–1936)
- ♣ Walter de la Mare (1873–1956)

163

CATS IN FILM TITLES
WORDSEARCH

T	H	E	C	A	T	R	E	T	U	R	N	S	O	N
U	F	C	O	P	E	L	P	O	E	P	T	A	C	H
O	R	W	A	F	E	L	I	X	T	H	X	M	Q	S
L	I	O	A	T	A	C	N	R	A	D	T	A	H	T
L	T	E	N	T	S	H	A	N	D	R	Y	T	I	A
A	Z	M	O	A	N	A	M	O	W	T	A	C	I	C
B	T	S	G	C	Q	U	N	K	B	C	V	R	Y	O
T	H	T	J	E	U	A	V	D	K	R	I	M	O	T
A	E	A	T	H	E	T	I	C	D	R	O	O	D	S
C	M	C	O	T	A	T	A	C	P	O	T	I	N	I
M	O	E	T	Z	Y	L	V	C	Q	U	G	R	T	R
R	O	G	H	F	T	B	U	L	H	Y	N	W	S	Q	A
W	G	T	R	I	B	L	A	C	K	P	R	U	U	E
A	A	E	Y	R	T	O	P	C	U	R	O	U	G	H
C	H	E	E	F	E	L	I	X	T	H	E	C	A	T

Cats have appeared in many film titles, usually amusingly. Here, fourteen of them can be found in this wordsearch – can you spot them?

- Black Cat
- Cat
- Cat Ballou
- Cat People
- Cats and Dogs
- Catwoman
- Copycat

- Felix the Cat
- Fritz the Cat
- That Darn Cat
- The Aristocats
- The Cat Returns
- The Cat's Meow
- Top Cat

164

FILM FAME

What is the name of the 1961 film starring André Morell and Barbara Shelley in which a woman is murdered and her cat takes dreadful revenge on the killers?

❧ *Feline Fortitude*
❧ *Keep on Clawing*
❧ *Shadow of Your Smile*
❧ *Stay in the Shadows*
❧ *The Shadow of the Cat*

165

WISDOM OF LIFE

Can you complete the quote from the American novelist and short-story writer Henry James (1843–1916)?

Cats and monkeys – monkeys and cats...

166

FELINE RIDDLE

Can you work out this riddle?

As I was going to St Ives,
I met a man with seven wives,
Each wife had seven sacks,
Each sack had seven cats,
Each cat had seven kits.
Kits, cats, sacks, and wives —
How many were going to St Ives?

167

DARK THOUGHTS

Who said: 'By night, all cats are grey'?

♣ Miguel de Cervantes (1547–1616)
♣ Alexandre Dumas (1802–1870)
♣ Henry Fielding (1707–1754)
♣ Victor Hugo (1802–1885)
♣ William Makepeace Thackeray (1811–1863)

168

SINGED PAW

In *The Monkey and the Cat* by Jean de La Fontaine, a monkey called Bertrand persuades Raton, a cat, to pull roasted chestnuts from the fire, promising him a share. As Raton retrieves them, burning his paw, Bertrand quickly eats them. A maid disturbs them and Raton gets nothing. What well-known phrase developed from this story?

❧ Being someone's cat's paw
❧ Know your partner
❧ Beware of the maid
❧ Don't pull chestnuts out of a fire

169

TIMELESS

Who said: 'Time spent with cats is never wasted'?

❧ Sidonie-Gabrielle Colette (1873–1954)
❧ George Eliot (1819–1880)
❧ Jean Ingelow (1820–1897)
❧ Charles Kingsley (1819–1875)

170

EGYPTIAN JUMBLEY

Hairless and with very large and open ears, especially wide at their base, this breed is highly distinctive. Can you find it in this jumbley?

PYXSHN

171

AS AN EMPEROR

Who wrote this poem?

> *Cruel, but composed and bland,*
> *Dumb, inscrutable and grand,*
> *So Tiberius might have sat,*
> *Had Tiberius been a cat.*

♣ Matthew Arnold (1822–1888)
♣ Thomas Moore (1779–1852)
♣ Thomas Nashe (1567–1601)
♣ Walt Whitman (1819–1892)

PAIRING UP

Can you pair up these twenty breeds with the dates when they originated?

Abyssinian	Pre-1800s
American Bobtail	Pre-1700s
Bengal	1950s
Bombay	1950s
Californian Spangled	1960s
Cornish Rex	1971
Devon Rex	1964
Egyptian Mau	1930s
European Burmese	1960s
Japanese Bobtail	1983
Korat	1860s
La Perm	1990s
Ocicat	1950s
Oriental Shorthair	1960s
Pixiebob	1982
Siamese	1975
Singapura	1966
Sphynx	Pre-1700s
Spotted Mist	1960s
Tonkinese	1975

173

FITTING END

Can you complete these lines by Alexander Pope (1688–1744)?

But thousands die, without or this or that,
Die, and...

174

KEEP SMILING!

In Lewis Carroll's story *Alice in Wonderland* there is a creature that has the ability to vanish at will, its grin being the last thing to go. What is its name?

♣ Luke the Leery
♣ Sidney the Smiler
♣ The Cheshire Cat
♣ The Cream-faced Cat
♣ The Diminishing Cat

175

BOATING REBUS

Edward Lear (1812–1888), while living in Italy, was inspired by his cat Foss to write a magical boating verse. Can you detect it in this puzzle?

THE   AND THE

176

COMIC JUMBLEY

A comic strip about a cat, created by cartoonist George Herriman, was published daily in America between 1913 and 1944. Can you see the cat's name in this puzzle?

RAKZY TAK

177

HOLE IN THE WALL!

Superstitions have embraced cats for thousands of years. One example was that if a cat's body was built into a house it would keep rodents away. When is it thought that this habit ceased?

   ❧ Fifteenth century
   ❧ Sixteenth century
   ❧ Seventeenth century
   ❧ Eighteenth century
   ❧ Nineteenth century

178

IN HARMONY?

The popular *Die Katzensymphonie* (Cat Symphony) by Austrian Moritz von Schwind (1804–1871) captures the rich and varied tones of cats, but when was it written?

   ❧ 1838
   ❧ 1848
   ❧ 1858
   ❧ 1868

DARK AND SILENT

In 1927, a now legendary silent horror film was screened, based on a story by the American playwright John Willard (1885–1942). It influenced subsequent films and has been reshot several times. Can you see the answer in this picture?

IN A FLAP!

Which famous scientist invented the cat flap so he would not be disturbed by his cats' comings and goings?

❧ Sir Alec Issigonis (1906–1988)
❧ Isambard Kingdom Brunel (1806–1859)
❧ Sir Henry Royce (1863–1933)
❧ George Stephenson (1781–1848)
❧ Sir Isaac Newton (1642–1727)
❧ Sir Barnes Wallis (1887–1979)

181

DEATH WISH

Francesco Petrarch (1304–1374), famous for his style of sonnet, loved his cat above anything or anyone. On Petrarch's death, what happened to his cat?

❧ It died from a broken heart
❧ It lived in luxury for the rest of its life
❧ Petrarch's heir turned it out onto the street
❧ It was put to death and mummified

182

EPICUREAN DELIGHTS

Dr Samuel Johnson (1709–1784), of English dictionary fame, had a cat he spoiled by feeding it oysters and other luxury treats. What was the name of the cat?

❧ Fancy
❧ Georgie
❧ Her Ladyship
❧ Hodge
❧ Tulip

WILD CATS NATIVE TO EUROPE, THE MIDDLE EAST AND NORTH AMERICA WORDSEARCH

E	U	R	A	S	I	A	N	L	Y	N	X	E	J	J
U	U	Q	U	I	R	L	A	K	X	S	W	U	R	A
R	U	R	B	B	V	M	T	R	E	T	N	I	U	G
A	I	S	O	L	U	X	N	Y	L	G	X	S	B	U
S	U	P	B	P	O	S	P	M	L	N	O	N	Z	A
I	N	A	C	R	E	A	B	E	Y	M	A	N	C	R
A	I	N	A	C	L	A	C	L	Y	M	E	S	T	U
M	O	I	T	N	S	A	N	D	C	A	T	I	O	N
L	N	S	Q	U	T	A	X	W	B	M	W	P	O	D
Y	I	H	U	S	I	X	T	B	I	O	M	A	L	I
M	A	L	E	D	I	U	O	I	O	L	B	R	M	N
X	Z	Y	A	E	R	T	L	L	K	J	D	D	H	F
T	Q	N	S	U	I	P	E	N	Y	C	O	C	O	A
C	A	X	Y	N	E	L	C	O	J	A	G	U	A	R
C	N	Z	D	R	A	P	O	E	L	R	I	D	R	T

The range of wild cats native to Europe, the Middle East and North America is wide. Twelve of them are featured in this wordsearch – how many can you spot?

- ♣ Bobcat
- ♣ Canadian Lynx
- ♣ Eurasian Lynx
- ♣ European Wildcat
- ♣ Jaguar
- ♣ Jaguarundi

- ♣ Jungle Cat
- ♣ Leopard
- ♣ Ocelot
- ♣ Puma
- ♣ Sandcat
- ♣ Spanish Lynx

184

GARDEN JUMBLEY

In his will, the Sultan El Daher Beybars, Ruler of Egypt and Syria in the thirteenth century, bequeathed a garden in Cairo for the support of homeless cats. They are still fed there at afternoon prayer time and cats from all over the city come for food. What is the garden's name (in English)?

TASC ROARDCH

185

GAME ON

Can you identify the name of a popular string game?

♣ Cat's Claw
♣ Cat's Cord
♣ Cat's Cradle
♣ Cat's Crib

186

ENCHANTING JUMBLEY

A French composer collaborated with Colette to write the opera *L'enfant et les Sortilèges* (The Child and the Enchantments). Within the opera there is a bravura cat duet sung by the Tom Cat and the She Cat. Can you see the composer's name in this puzzle?

REAMUIC SPHOEJ VELAR

187

FELINE INSPIRATION

What did the Polish composer Frédéric Chopin (1810–1849) do when his cat walked across the keyboard?

❧ Banned it from his room
❧ Liked the melody and wrote 'The Cat Waltz' around it
❧ Trapped it under the piano's lid

WILD CATS NATIVE TO SOUTH AMERICA WORDSEARCH

A wide and varied range of wild cats are native to South America. Eight of them are featured in this wordsearch – how many can you spot?

S	P	Y	O	C	E	L	O	T	J
D	R	A	J	A	G	U	A	A	A
O	C	E	M	I	M	U	G	Y	G
K	O	D	K	P	M	U	V	Q	U
D	O	K	D	O	A	S	P	I	A
O	S	M	I	R	T	S	I	U	R
K	S	H	U	M	A	N	C	A	T
S	A	N	P	M	A	R	G	A	Y
P	D	O	K	S	I	R	G	I	T
I	T	A	C	R	E	G	I	T	S

❧ Jaguar
❧ Jaguarundi
❧ Kodkod
❧ Margay

❧ Ocelot
❧ Pampas Cat
❧ Puma
❧ Tiger Cat

189

CATS AND DOGS

There is a saying: 'There are more ways of killing a dog than hanging him.' What is an equivalent involving a cat? It begins:

There is more...

190

SILENT INVADER

What would you call a villain who works with stealth? Can you spot it in this picture puzzle?

PREMONITIONS

A famous therapy cat living in a nursing home on Rhode Island, USA, would visit patients, sniffing and observing them. At times he would curl up and sleep with particular people, who then died within a few hours. Can you name the cat?

❧ Arthur
❧ Beau Brummell
❧ Goodbye
❧ Lamplighter
❧ Oscar

❦

LOST CHORD?

The composer Andrew Lloyd Webber lost the entire score to a sequel to *The Phantom of the Opera* when, in 2007, his six-month old Turkish Van cat stepped on his keyboard and wiped the score from his computer. What was the cat's four-letter palindromic name?

❦

CERTAINLY SUPERB

In North America the term 'the cat's pyjamas' is used to describe a person who is dressed to perfection. What is the equivalent of this in the UK?

❧ The cat's blaze
❧ The cat's coat
❧ The cat's ears
❧ The cat's nose
❧ The cat's paws
❧ The cat's whiskers

KITTEN ON THE KEYS!

Composer Domenico Scarlatti (1685–1757) had a cat that composed a fugue! The cat liked prancing on his harpsichord and wrote 'Fugue in G Minor, L. 499'. Scarlatti may have helped a little, but the first few bars, at least, are convincingly the work of a cat. What was the cat's name?

CELLIUNLPA

MUSICAL *CATS* WORDSEARCH

B	U	S	T	O	P	H	E	R	J	O	N	E	S	O
O	R	E	G	G	U	T	M	U	T	M	U	R	L	S
J	E	N	N	Y	A	N	Y	D	O	T	S	D	Y	K
R	O	U	E	N	C	O	P	S	Q	S	D	I	G	N
U	O	P	N	I	T	Y	U	J	X	E	P	U	R	A
M	A	Y	G	O	R	G	O	N	U	Z	Q	U	I	H
P	A	K	L	A	A	R	E	T	E	U	C	U	Z	S
E	M	C	M	R	I	D	E	Q	U	I	P	L	A	E
L	P	A	A	Z	J	R	V	J	M	L	L	E	B	L
T	P	P	I	V	O	N	O	Z	O	W	Q	U	E	B
E	S	W	Z	N	I	P	N	T	R	G	U	K	L	M
A	P	R	O	U	Q	T	L	G	C	O	N	O	L	I
Z	I	M	A	N	X	N	Y	W	M	I	P	U	A	K
E	Y	G	R	I	Z	A	B	L	L	Y	V	Q	M	S
R	S	E	E	L	E	F	F	O	T	S	I	M	R	M

Many cats appeared in *Cats*, composed by Andrew Lloyd Webber and based on *Old Possum's Book of Practical Cats* by T. S. Eliot. Twelve of them are in this wordsearch puzzle – how many can you spot?

❧ Asparagus
❧ Bustopher Jones
❧ Grizabella
❧ Jennyanydots
❧ Macavity
❧ Mr Mistoffelees

❧ Mungojerrie
❧ Old Deuteronomy
❧ Rumpelteazer
❧ Rum Tum Tugger
❧ Skimbleshanks
❧ Victoria

196

ABOUT TURN

What is the cat-related term for what is done by a turncoat, a person who changes sides when trouble and conflict are about to happen?

♣ To cat about
♣ To cat creep
♣ To cat vamp
♣ To turn cat about
♣ To turn cat-in-pan

❧

197

SCOTTISH PREFERENCES

Female cats are known as queens and male cats as toms in Britain, but what have they also been known as in Scotland? Can you detect them in these jumbleys?

Female: ODE
Male: BIG

❧

GIANT AMONG PROTECTIONISTS

Cleveland Amory (1917–1998) was a board director of the Humane Society of the United States, founder of the Fund for Animals, and President of the New England Anti-Vivisection Society (NEAVS) from 1997 to 1998. However, he is possibly best known for books about his cat whom he rescued from New York streets on Christmas Eve 1977. What was the cat's name?

❧ Broadway
❧ Brooklyn
❧ Madison
❧ Polar Bear

MEN AT RISK

What is the cat-related saying used when a man is dominated by a woman?

❧ To be cat-pecked
❧ To live under a cat's foot
❧ To suffer from a cat's miaow

WORD-SPOT

The Latin name for domestic cats is *Felis silvestris catus*. How many words (each of at least three letters) can you make out of the Latin name, other than 'cat'? At least 66 are possible, and these are given in the answers.

ANSWERS

❧

1: PAIRING UP
🐾 Marilyn Monroe – Mitsou
🐾 Iris Murdoch – General Butchkin
🐾 Florence Nightingale – Mr Bismarck
🐾 Nostradamus – Grimalkin
🐾 George Sand – Minou

2: INSPIRATIONAL JUMBLEY
🐾 Jellylorum

3: DOMESTICATED CATS
🐾 7,000 years

4: BREED PUZZLE
🐾 Ragdoll

5: REMARKABLE VISION
🐾 285 degrees

6: BRAIN CAPACITY
🐾 1 per cent

7: ANCESTRY
🐾 Eleven million

8: AVERTING DANGER
🐾 Twelve

P				N			P	A	L	F	T	A			C
	E				E							G			
		T				U						N			
		L	I	T	T	E	R	T	R	A	Y		I		
			N				E					M			
		T	E	K	S	A	B			R		O			
	L				U					I		O			
C	W			W		R					N	R			
	O			O			A					G			
	B	L		R				N							
			L	M	I	C	R	O	C	H	I	P			
			A	E					E						
			R												
	F	L	E	A	S	P	R	A	Y						
I	D	E	N	T	I	T	Y	D	I	S	C				

10: SACRED FELINE
♣ Birman

11: STEPPE JUMBLEY
♣ Russian Blue

12: FELINE PULSE RATE
♣ 110 to 140

13: SAFER DRIVING
♣ 1933

14: IMPRESSIVE ATHLETE
♣ Seven

15: ROCK JUMBLEY
♣ Freddie Mercury

16: POPULAR NURSERY RHYME
♣ *I frightened a little mouse under her chair.*

17: FRENCH CONNECTION
♣ Marie Antoinette

18: CAT-FISH JUMBLEY
♣ Alexander Borodin

19: TONGUE-TESTING JUMBLEY
♣ Mark Twain

20: PRIVILEGED GIFT
♣ James Dean

21: SPOT THE DIFFERENCE

22: CLASSIC ANIMATION
❧ Top Cat (TC)

23: TOURIST TROPHY CAT
❧ Manx Cat

24: TREASURED COMPANION
❧ Charles Dickens

25: SOCIAL SKILLS
❧ Lion

34: CAT BREEDS SPIDERMITE CROSSWORD

35: CHARTWELL FAVOURITE
♣ Jock

36: MISSION IMPOSSIBLE?
♣ *Belling the Cat*

37: TRAGIC END
♣ Drowned in a goldfish bowl

38: REVENGE ATTACK
♣ Hinse

39: HEART BREAKING
♣ Thomas Hardy

40: EUROPEAN LEGACY
♣ The Romans

41: PAIRING UP
♣ Bobcat − *Felis lynx rufus*
♣ Canada Lynx − *Felis lynx canadensis*
♣ Mountain Cat − *Felis jacobita*
♣ Ocelot − *Felis pardalis*
♣ Pampas Cat − *Felis colocolo*
♣ Puma − *Felis concolor*

42: RARE BREED JUMBLEY
❧ Khmer

43: PAIRING UP
Fishing Cat – *Felis prionailurus viverrinus*
Iberian Lynx – *Felis lynx pardina*
Marbled Cat – *Felis pardofelis marmorata*
Pallas' Cat – *Felis manul*
Sand Cat – *Felis margarita*
Serval – *Felis serval*

44: SHORT-HAIRED CAT JUMBLEY
Abyssinian

45: SAYING HELLO
❧ Kingsley Amis

46: FABLE REBUS
❧ *The Lion, the Fox and the Beasts*

47: WITH MENACES!
❧ Hot Dog

48: FELINE WISDOM
❧ Jeff Valdez

49: MAGNETIC FORCE
❧ Catmint

	S	C	O	T	T	I	S	H	F	O	L	D		C
S		A				A								O
E		R	S			V							C	R
L	O		I		E		A				I			N
K	I		N		S		N			C				I
I	R		G		E		A	A						S
R	K		A		M			T						H
K	K		P		R			M						R
R	R		U	R	U	S	S	I	A	N	B	L	U	E
E	R		B			I		L						X
X	A	E				A		A				N		
	N				M		Y		A					
		G				E		A			M			
	A					S		N						
L	I	A	T	B	O	B	E	S	E	N	A	P	A	J

51: A PASSING OMEN
♣ A stranger is coming

52: DEATH PENALTY JUMBLEY
♣ Bastet

53: PAIRING UP
Black cat (Britain) – Good luck
Black cat (North America) – Bad luck
Black-white-grey mixture – Good luck
Stray tortoiseshell cat – Misfortune
White cat (most countries) – Bad luck

54: CAT ADAGE
♣ *... cat dragged in*

67: SPOT THE DIFFERENCE

Dr. Seuss

68: COLOUR REBUS
♣ Van Pattern

69: FIRST KITTENS
♣ Abraham Lincoln

70: CATWOMAN JUMBLEY
♣ Eartha Kitt

71: HIGH FLYER
♣ Patsy

72: MORE THAN A LODGER
♣ T. S. Eliot

73: ORDER, ORDER!
♣ H. G. Wells

74: FISHY NATURE
Porgy and Bess

75: LITERARY MERCENARY
The Dogs of War

76: ROMAN REBUS
Cato (Marcus Porcius Cato)

77: GUT WRENCHING!
Catgut

78: THEATRICAL DISPLEASURE
Catcalls

79: BURNING DESIRE
Pericles, Prince of Tyre

80: LONG-HAIRED BREEDS WORDSEARCH

E	S	E	N	A	V	A	J				N			
	I								A					
	B				C			M				E		
	E			A	Y			R				I		
	R			R	M	A	I	N	E	C	O	O	N	
	I		O		R	B		L					A	
	A	G			I		L		A		P	F		
	N				C	O			M		E	F		
A	F				D					O	R	I		
N	O	R	W	E	G	I	A	N	F	O	R	E	S	T
	R		A									I		
	E		R			E	S	E	N	I	L	A	B	
	S											N		
	T													
A	M	E	R	I	C	A	N	C	U	R	L			

81: MODEL PARADE
♣ Catwalk

82: SOUND ONLY
♣ Cat's whisker

83: CATS' PLEDGE
♣ Natchez, Mississippi

84: FELINE COMPANY
♣ Robert E. Lee

85: PAIRING UP
Cat continuously sneezes – Indicates rain
Cat cries as you leave home – Unlucky
Cat licks its tail – Expect a light shower
Cat sneezes once – Lucky for the household
Cat sneezes thrice – Everyone catches a cold
Cat with its back to a fire – Storm to come
Cat washing in a doorway – Visiting clergyman
Cat scratches a table leg – Change in the weather
Cat washes its face and ears – Long, wet period

86: LORD MAYOR'S CAT
♣ Dick Whittington

87: HOME FROM HOME
♣ Edward Lear

88: WATERY REBUS
♣ Fishing Cat

89: ITALIAN FREEDOM
♣ At her feet

97: DOG ASSOCIATION
☙ Devon Rex

98: TALKATIVE JUMBLEY
☙ Tobermory

99: POLITICAL LEADERS
☙ Cat Mandu

100: SENSITIVE DESCRIPTION
☙ Rudyard Kipling

101: HYBRID JUMBLEY
☙ Tonkinese

102: TOUCH OF GINGER
☙ Orlando

103: UPDATED NURSERY RHYME
☙ *Little Tommy Stout.*

104: EARLY TAMING
☙ African Wildcat

105: WILD CATS SPIDERMITE CROSSWORD

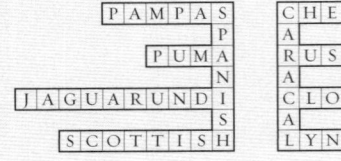
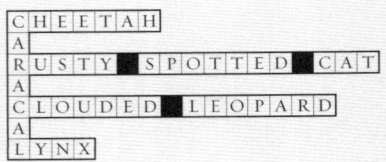

106: NAVAL CAT
☙ *HMS Amethyst*

107: EAR JUMBLEY
❧ Scottish Fold

108: SHIP'S CAT HONOURED
❧ Able Seaman Simon

109: STUMPY TAIL JUMBLEY
❧ Japanese Bobtail

110: WILD CAT PUZZLE
❧ Sand Cat

111: NO PLACE LIKE HOME
❧ Mark Twain

112: PAIRING UP
❧ Aesop (c.620–560 BC) – Devious and cunning

❧ Pliny (AD 23–79) – Associated with lust

❧ Plutarch (AD c.46–120) – Clean (noting that unnatural odours could make them mad)

113: HOMESPUN WISDOM
❧ *... the meat is out of reach*

114: PAINFUL RESULT
❧ Cat o' nine tails

115: CRAMPED STYLE
❧ No room to swing a cat

116: LITERARY JUMBLEY
❧ *Puss in Boots*

117: CAT CLOCK!
🍀 First Witch in *Macbeth*

118: HEINOUS ACT
🍀 Cat and Mouse Act

119: ROCKY SITUATION
🍀 *... in a room full of rocking chairs*

120: MUSICAL FELINE
🍀 *Look What the Cat Dragged In*

121: PAIRING UP
🍀 Cat – *CatDog*
🍀 Chance (T-Bone) – *SWAT Kats*
🍀 Salem Saberhagen – *Sabrina, the Teenage Witch*
🍀 Spot – *Star Trek: The Next Generation*
🍀 The Cat – *Red Dwarf*

122: WILD CATS NATIVE TO AFRICA AND ASIA WORDSEARCH

	C	H	E	E	T	A	H		L	A	V	R	E	S
					R		A		C					N
				E			C							O
	J	U	N	G	L	E	C	A	T					W
F			I				R							L
I		T					A							E
S	L	E	O	P	A	R	D	C						O
H			T	A										P
I			A		L							W		A
N		T	A	C	D	E	L	B	R	A	M	I		R
G			D			A					L			D
C		L	N				S			D				
A	I		A					C		C				
T	O		S						A	A				
N	B	O	R	N	E	A	N	B	A	Y	C	A	T	

123: LIMITATIONS
♣ Convent

124: ALMOST DEITY
♣ *... Cats have never forgotten this.*

125: PAIRING UP
♣ Bagheera – Rudyard Kipling (*The Jungle Book*)
♣ Cheshire Cat – Lewis Carroll (*Alice in Wonderland*)
♣ Crookshanks – J. R. Rowling (Harry Potter books)
♣ Smiley Cat – Dr Seuss (*The Cat in the Hat*)
♣ Tom Kitten – Beatrix Potter

126: JOYS OF LIFE
♣ Music and cats

127: PLUM PROBLEM
♣ Have no tact

128: INEVITABLE OUTCOME
♣ *... it becomes a cat*

129: PAIRING UP
♣ Eureka – *The Wizard of Oz*
♣ Figaro – *Pinocchio*
♣ Ginger – *The Chronicles of Narnia*
♣ Graymalkin – *Macbeth*
♣ Kitty – *Little House on the Prairie*
♣ Mr Bigglesworth – *Austin Powers*

130: PLAYFUL NATURE
♣ *... must expect to be scratched*

131: EARLY HERO JUMBLEY
♣ Crimean Tom

132: CHILDREN'S LITERATURE
Then you shall have no pie.

133: ANIMAL EGALITARIANISM!
I like pigs. Dogs look up to us. Cats look down on us. Pigs treat us as equals.

134: ARTISTIC INSIGHT
Pablo Picasso

135: HIDDEN CREATIVITY
Abraham Lincoln

136: IRISH INSPIRATION
... His changing eyes.

137: CATS, GAMES AND COMICS
Big – *Sonic Adventure*
Cait Smith – *Final Fantasy VII*
Catbert – *Dilbert*
Chubby Huggs – *Get Fuzzy*

138: PERCEPTIVE VIEWPOINT
Leonardo da Vinci

139: AMERICAN TWIST
Curiosity killed the cat

140: FOLKLORE PUZZLE
When the cat's away, the mice will play

141: WHO'S THE TOY?
Michel de Montaigne

142: LUNAR LUNACY
Played the fiddle

143: LUCKY LEGACY
♣ Tiddles

144: FAMILY FORTUNES
♣ *Two Gentlemen of Verona*

145: SALTY ENDEAVOUR
♣ *... sees the shore*

146: WITCHES' CATS SPIDERMITE CROSSWORD

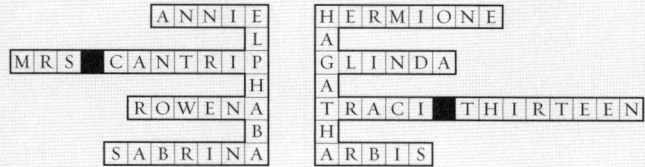

147: DIRE RESULTS
♣ Put a cat among the pigeons

148: RELIGIOUS INTOLERANCE
♣ No cats to kill rats

149: MEDIEVAL SAYING
♣ cat was let out of the bag

150: BREED REBUS
♣ Korat

151: SNOOZE TIME
♣ Catnap

152: NEW FOR OLD
♣ Ram

163: CATS IN FILM TITLES WORDSEARCH

T	H	E	C	A	T	R	E	T	U	R	N	S	
U	C			E	L	P	O	E	P	T	A	C	
O	W	A											S
L	O		T	A	C	N	R	A	D	T	A	H	T
L			T	S						T		A	
A		M	A	N	A	M	O	W	T	A	C		C
B		S	C			N			C				O
T		T	E			D	K						T
A		A	H		T		C	D					S
C		C	T		T	A	C	P	O	T			I
	E	Z		L		C			G				R
	H	T	B			Y				S			A
	T	I				P							E
	A	R						O					H
C			F	E	L	I	X	T	H	E	C	A	T

164: FILM FAME
♣ *The Shadow of the Cat*

165: WISDOM OF LIFE
♣ *... all human life is there!'*

166: FELINE RIDDLE
♣ Only one – the narrator

167: DARK THOUGHTS
♣ Miguel de Cervantes

168: SINGED PAW
♣ Being someone's cat's paw

E	U	R	A	S	I	A	N	L	Y	N	X		J	J
	U					A						U		A
		R	B		M					N				G
		S	O		U			G	X					U
		P	B	P			L	N						A
		A	C		E		E	Y						R
		N	A		A	C	L							U
		I	T		S	A	N	D	C	A	T			N
		S		T	A		W							D
		H		I		T		I						I
		L		D		O			L					
		Y	A			L				D				
		N				E					C			
	A	X				C		J	A	G	U	A	R	
C			D	R	A	P	O	E	L					T

184: GARDEN JUMBLEY
❧ Cats' Orchard

185: GAME ON
❧ Cat's Cradle

186: ENCHANTING JUMBLEY
❧ Maurice Joseph Ravel (1875–1937)

187: FELINE INSPIRATION
❧ Liked the melody and wrote 'The Cat Waltz' around it

```
    P   O C E L O T J
D   A A         A A
O     M M   G     G
K       P U       U
D         A   P   A
O         R S     R
K     U       C
      N   M A R G A Y
    D               T
I T A C R E G I T
```

189: CATS AND DOGS
❧ *... than one way to skin a cat*

190: SILENT INVADER
❧ Cat burglar

191: PREMONITIONS
❧ Oscar

192: LOST CHORD?
❧ Otto

193: CERTAINLY SUPERB
❧ The cat's whiskers

194: KITTEN ON THE KEYS!
❧ Pulcinella

195: MUSICAL *CATS* WORDSEARCH

B	U	S	T	O	P	H	E	R	J	O	N	E	S	O
	R	E	G	G	U	T	M	U	T	M	U	R	L	S
J	E	N	N	Y	A	N	Y	D	O	T	S	D		K
R			E					S			D		G	N
U				I			U			E			R	A
M					R	G			U				I	H
P	A			A	A	R		T					Z	S
E		C		R	I		E						A	E
L			A			R		J					B	L
T		P		V	O		O		O				E	B
E	S			N	I			T		G			L	M
A			O			T			C		N		L	I
Z		M					Y			I		U	A	K
E	Y										V		M	S
R	S	E	E	L	E	F	F	O	T	S	I	M	R	M

196: ABOUT TURN
❧ To turn cat-in-pan

197: SCOTTISH PREFERNCES
❧ Female: Doe
❧ Male: Gib

198: GIANT AMONG PROTECTIONISTS
❧ Polar Bear

199: MEN AT RISK
❧ To live under a cat's foot

200: WORD-SPOT

alive	car	cart	cause	cave	Celt
cleave	crate	craves	crust	fast	fate
feast	feel	felt	festive	frail	lass
last	late	leaf	least	leave	less
lest	lie	live	liver	lives	lust
rail	rate	rats	rave	rest	rust
safe	sate	save	scat	seal	seer
self	sell	sever	silver	slate	slave
slaver	slit	star	start	stave	stress
strive	tail	tassel	teal	tear	trivial
trust	vast	vat	vault	veil	vest

... and many more

ABOUT PATRICIA KING

Patricia King is an established author, having co-authored a comprehensive puppy-and-dog book and written *The Dog Puzzler*, a sister volume to this Puzzler. Throughout her life, Patricia has gathered curious and practical information about cats, their habits and histories, and how they have become interwoven in literature, poetry and folklore. In this mind-stretching and fun-packed book, Patricia offers a way to get to know cats better.

Patricia has a BA (Hons) in English Language and Literature, together with an MA in Creative Writing and Authorship, and works in the library of an animal welfare organisation.